KETTERING

THEN AND NOW

Ian Addis

and

Robert Mercer

"There are places I remember all my life .... though some have changed"
John Lennon

JEMA PUBLICATIONS

Published 1997 by Jema Publications

© Ian Addis, Robert Mercer, Kettering Evening Telegraph

ISBN   1-871468-58-2

Publisher's Note
Every care has been taken in the preparation of this book and all the information has been carefully checked and is believed to be correct at the time of publication. However, neither the authors nor the publisher can accept responsibility for any errors or omissions or for any loss, damage, injury or inconvenience resulting from the use of this book.

Jema Publications
40 Ashley Lane
Moulton
Northampton
NN3 7TJ

Printed in Great Britain by Woolnough Bookbinding Ltd., Irthlingborough

ACKNOWLEDGEMENTS

We have received a great deal of assistance in the compilation of this book and wish to record our appreciation to everyone who has helped, notably Liz McBride and the staff at the Kettering Evening Telegraph, Malcolm Robinson (Kettering Public Library), Tony Ireson, Fred Mason, Robin Reeves, Norman Neal, Brian Liggins, J Fovargue, Derek Styman, Nigel Hanger, Ron Curtis and all who have made contributions, however small.

Kettering in the Nineteen Fifties

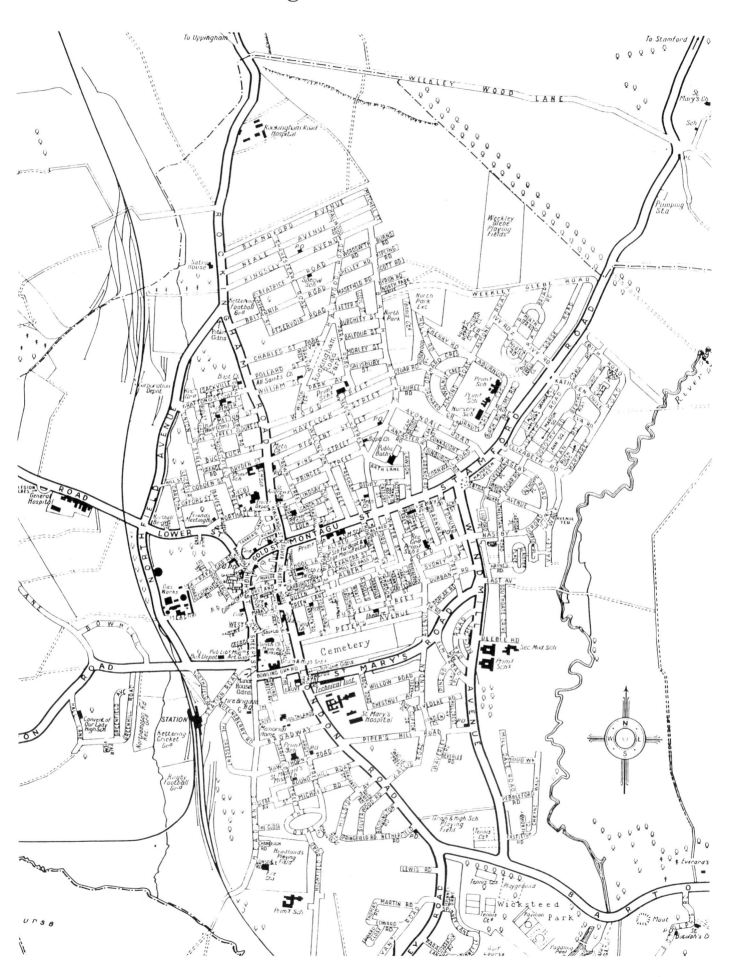

INTRODUCTION

A brief look at the map opposite reveals how relatively small Kettering was in the early nineteen fifties. Expansion had begun, with new estates springing up off Stamford Road, Pytchley Road, Northampton Road and Windmill Avenue, but the heart of the town, with its shops, markets, offices, factories, cinemas, pubs and chapels, still provided a focal point for activity.

As many people spent much of their lives in the same house, at the same workplace, digging the same garden field, relaxing at the same club or worshipping at the same church or chapel, there is little remarkable in my ability to recall vividly the families that lived in the street where I grew up. Nor were my childhood experiences - "newting up the pits", Saturday morning pictures, watching the 'Poppies', trainspotting at Glendon bridge, Sunday evening band concerts at the Pleasure Park, the occasional fish and chip supper at Beetson's - so very different from those enjoyed by countless others at that time.

But times change, and so do places.

'*Kettering, Then and Now*' presents contrasting views of the town and neighbouring locations, many distanced by some forty years, and provides both long-time residents and 'incomers' with an interesting perspective on the many developments that have taken place over that period.

Ian Addis

For me, the making of this book was nothing less than a small world revealed through a camera viewfinder. I was privileged to explore it with Ian and thereby share his enthusiasms for Kettering. I delighted in his stories, insights and anecdotes of the people and places of his youth which, being of the same generation, often paralleled my own experiences of boyhood in another town in a very different place.

Despite a becoming modesty it must be recognised that Ian shows a remarkable ability to recall names, places and events from the past. I only arrived in Kettering in the early seventies, but even in my time in the town much has disappeared or been radically altered. We both relished the challenge of recording and reflecting on these changes and it has been stimulating to share the task of fusing together text and photographs, hopefully creating a rich pattern of information and reminiscence.

I dedicate my share of our endeavours to all those lovely people who made me welcome and whom I now know as friends.

Robert Mercer

August 1997

A row of terraced houses in Northall Street c1955.

CONTENTS

Acknowledgements iii

Map of Kettering in the Nineteen Fifties iv

Introduction v

Contents vii

Map of Town Centre Route A to S viii

Plates 1 to 22 1

The Centenary of the Evening Telegraph 23

Kettering General Hospital Centenary 29

Plates 33 to 53 33

Where are they? 54

Index 55

Bibliography 56

KETTERING TOWN CENTRE

The first half of this book focuses upon changes to the town centre. Sites recorded in sequence A to S are shown on the town plan below enabling readers to follow the route and note the comparisons for themselves.

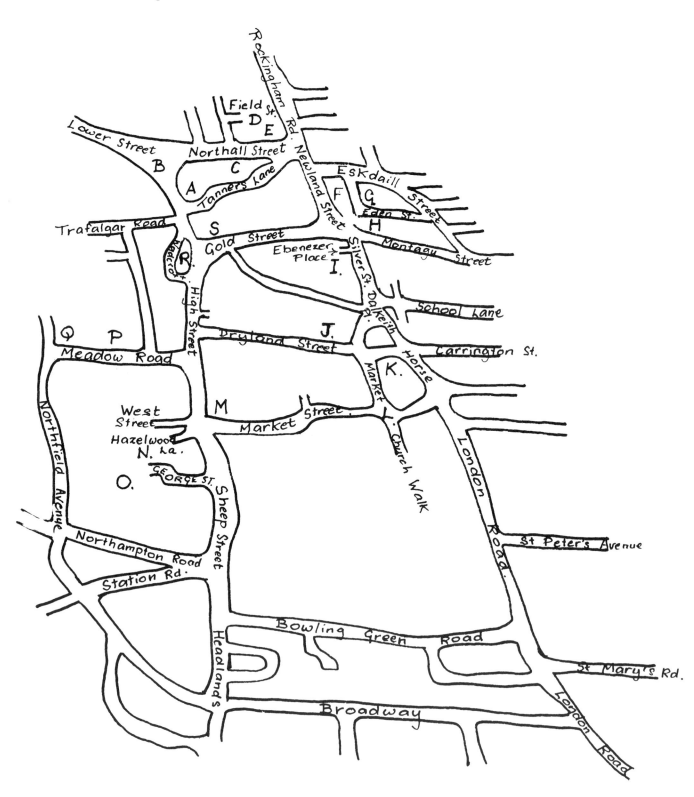

Jasmine House -
demolished 1962 'to widen and improve Lower Street'.

The garish advertising hoarding now dominating the corner of Tanners Lane and Lower Street is a poor substitute for the elegant three-storeyed, double-fronted building that formerly occupied the site. It is possible that during the 1850s Jasmine House was home to Thomas Henry Gotch, son of the celebrated John Cooper Gotch, who had run both the family's leather and shoemaking businesses and the Gotch Bank. Later it was occupied by the Steff family who, between 1882 and 1923, produced the 'Kettering Guardian' and numerous other publications on the premises, under the auspices of the local Conservative party.

The wooden gate under the arch in the stone wall in Tanners Lane was originally the back entrance to Deene House, whose frontage is hidden behind the imposing facade of the Elworthy Brewery maltings in Lower Street. The house itself is currently the home of Fred Mason, a highly respected restorer of antique furniture and a member of the famous Kettering bowling family. Now an entrance to Roger's Furniture Market, the white shop front in Lower Street was formerly Annie Freeman's sweetshop and cafe, while the windows of the 'High Quality Footwear' store next door have long since been bricked up. Keen eyed observers may note the sign on the wall of Jasmine House which points down Trafalgar Road to the Army Information Centre, once sited on the Fleet Street corner opposite the Aquascutum factory.

B

Lower Street Triangle

Of the major buildings flanking the complex network of traffic lights at the inter-section of Lower Street and Northall Street only two have survived the dramatic redevelopment that has so transformed the area. The Three Cocks Inn and the distinctive Quaker Chapel, (Friends Meeting House), are still clearly identifiable, but the heavily built-up triangle, fronted by the handsome white painted Wayman's Bakery, (formerly Warwicker's), and backed by East's imposing Victorian boot and shoe factory in Northall Street, has long since disappeared.

The rows of houses in Upper Street, to the right of the baker's shop, and Lower Street to the left, together with Frank Elks' garage, a grocer's and a shoe repairer's, were demolished in 1958 along with the rest of the site. The factory, however, latterly occupied by the Walker Last Company, remained until 1984 when it was pulled down to make way for flats for the elderly in Windsor Gardens.

This aerial photograph, taken in June 1983, clearly shows the overgrown two and a half acre site behind the factory, flanked by Bayes Street, Oxford Street and Carlton Street, which once belonged to Jacques and Son, the florist and market gardener.

Charles East's factory, first opened in 1862, and extended several times during the late 19th century, had housed the first boot closing machines to be used in Kettering. There was widespread opposition to their use, organised by an anti-machinery movement, but East persevered recognising the benefits the innovation would eventually bring to the working people of the town.

C

Kettering Textiles

A small group of interested and expectant onlookers watch the fire-engines arrive at Stocks leather dressers factory in Northall Street. The 'S' still visible over the doorway above the sign of its current occupants, Kettering Textiles, formerly Plaistere and Hanger, refers to the original owner, JT Stockburn, who built it as a corset factory. To the left of the fine stone Victorian industrial building was the Northall Street/Tanners Lane complex. In the fifties this notable area of old Kettering still bustled with life. Among the more familiar buildings were Grensell's electrical contractors, the underground public toilets opposite Jack Cross' newsagents, the Waggon and Horses pub, the former North End National School, (latterly the St Andrew's Institute), and the Lindrea leather warehouse. Nearly all were swept away to facilitate road widening and town development except the warehouse, which escaped the bulldozer only to be destroyed by fire in May 1975.

At the time of writing Kettering Textiles plan a move to new premises and uncertainty surrounds the fate of their former building as the whole site is scheduled for a new shopping complex.

D

Field Street Avenue

Although almost seventy years separate these views of Field Street Avenue, there are few significant differences until the eye focuses upon the huge structures rising at the bottom of the road in the older photograph. They are the wooden cooling towers of the Kettering Corporation Electricity Works which had opened in Dickman's Meadow, off Rockingham Road, in May 1904. By 1911 it was not only lighting Kettering's main streets but also burning the town's rubbish in its refuse incinerator. A valued by-product of the cooling towers was the sulphur baths, the dubious delights of which town historian Tony Ireson recalls sampling. The baths were widely used by locals in a bid to 'kill off' scabies. The towers were demolished in August 1958, several years before the closure of the electricity works itself whose social club, with its snooker table, skittles, dominoes and Dansette record player had proved a mecca for us youngsters in the late fifties. After moving to a new home in Eskdaill Street, the club finally closed down due to lack of support as recently as 1995.

The roof of the Sainsbury supermarket complex, which now occupies the entire site of the electricity works, can be seen in the modern photograph.

E

Northall Street

Newcomers to Kettering will have difficulty in identifying the location of the older photograph. The empty site in the foreground was previously occupied by a row of buildings which stretched almost the entire length of Northall Street from Rockingham Road down to Bayes Street (see page vi). Demolition began in 1958, but the site remained largely undeveloped for many years until the wholesale regeneration of the area in the seventies and the eventual construction of the vast Sainsbury's complex from which the car on the right of the modern photograph is emerging. It is staggering to recall just how much of old Kettering's enterprise and endeavour disappeared with this inevitable demolition. The supermarket, with its service station and carpark, now covers the site formerly occupied by, amongst others, the Electricity Board Works in Rockingham Road, the Town Band club, the Hare and Hounds and the Vine public houses, Blackett's corner, Jack Cross' newsagents shop, the Central Printing Works, a row of terraced houses, a courtyard behind known as Spring Gardens and fronted by the pub of the same name, the former Salvation Army Citadel building in Field Street, and Larkinson's scrap metal premises where I spent many happy holidays working for the Carpenter brothers during the early sixties. Beyond the access to the supermarket carpark, on the Field Street corner which previously housed the obligatory outdoor beerhouse, a shrubbery thrives alongside the medical centre, relocated from its Dryland Street home in February 1990.

F

Newland Street

Newland Street remains a busy town centre thoroughfare as evidenced by the activity in the modern photograph. In the nineteen fifties, with traffic still travelling in both directions, pedestrians obviously felt safe enough to walk in the road while passing the demolition site previously occupied by the Fleur-de-Lys pub and Miles' fish and poultry shop, now housing the Argos store. The white painted building with the obligatory blinds is Ernest Lewin's Pork Butchers, currently Button Boutique, while the splendid three-storeyed Victorian edifaces near the clock are part of a row once devoted to the Kettering Cooperative Society. These buildings survive practically unscathed, although the gabled frontage of the former KICS Drapery dating from 1893 and pictured above the bus in the later photograph, has sadly lost much of its original elegance.

G

St Andrew's Street

St Andrew's School stood on the site now occupied by the Eskdaill Medical Centre, just across the road and in close proximity to the church of which it was very much part. Originally built towards the end of the last century it was eventually demolished in the early sixties, its pupils having transferred to the former Central School building in Grafton Street. The headteacher during the fifties was the redoubtable Miss Margaret A Rayson Smith, (MARS to her pupils), an idiosyncratic figure in those days with her severe hairstyle and tweed suits. The original playground wall, to the extreme right of the school photograph, still survives on the Eden Street side of the building. The area to the left, seen more fully in the photograph of FW Goodfellow's Leather Merchants factory, (middle opposite), was a smallholding and 'garden-field'. The site between Goodfellow's corner and Newland Street was occupied by KICS property, notably stables housing the horses that pulled the milk and bread carts on their daily rounds. There was also a row of shops, including a butcher's, fishmonger's and greengrocer's. Today the truncated pinnacles of the Newlands Centre dominate the skyline, while a constant stream of vehicles passes by on the inner ring road (right).

FW Goodfellow's factory, situated on the St Andrew's Street corner.

Montagu Corner (Woodcocks)

Oh bliss! In the fifties this was the site of Kettering's only set of traffic lights! A solitary van makes its way down Montagu Street past the heavily blinded ground floor windows of Edward Woodcock, General Draper. As the words on the first floor inform us, the shop also sold millinery, mantles, costumes and dresses, and was staffed by very smart sales girls, all adept at using the 'overhead railway' system to receive payment and give back change. Built in 1899, it later became part of the huge Co-op department store and is now an estate agents. Next door was Henry Barlow's bakery and restaurant. Only the metal support, from which hung the Mikado cafe sign, survives to provide a clue to its former use; however Phillips', Furnishers and Household Drapers continue trading from the adjoining building in Newland Street as they have for the past hundred years. Among the premises across the road were Walker's the jeweller, the Cooperative Permanent Building Society, Lillian Worrall milliner, Florence M Tomblin ladies' wear, H Winstone newsagent and tobacconist, the Normandie Restaurant and, on the first floor, the Cooperative and Labour Institute. Opposite Woodcock's, on the corner of Silver Street and Montagu Street, was Paul Taylor's radio and television shop. A family firm owned from the turn of the century by his father Harry, who had originally sold bicycles. Today, regrettably, it seems unable to find a permanent role to play in the commercial life of this busy corner of Kettering, and is currently unoccupied.

I

Ebenezer Place

There appears little difference about Ebenezer Place since the first photograph was taken some forty years ago, but the redesignated shop frontages reflect the changing times. Len Fleckney, an accomplished local billiards and snooker player, was then the proprietor of the long established family drapery stores. The premises has latterly had a somewhat chequered career having been Oscar's Pantry, offering baguettes and Spanish omelettes, and more recently a bric a brac shop. The tall building behind Fleckney's was once the National Telephone Co. Ltd. Public Call Office and the chapel-like edifice beyond, which now houses Clairy's Discount Store, was formerly a leather warehouse. A tree hides the narrow passage which many will remember as a useful short cut leading to Ivy's Cafe in Gold Street, while Campbell's Great National Furnishers has given way to the Supervision store.

Dryland Street

The unmistakable facade of Charnley the Opticians in the High Street provides an enduring perspective for the two views. Dryland Street was formerly known as Workhouse Lane until renamed in memory of the celebrated doctor who lived and worked from a practice originally situated in a stone house at the High Street end of the lane. The recently restored horse trough outside the library building in Sheep Street is another example of the town's affection for him. The surgery was eventually moved higher up the street and I can recall childhood visits to doctors Mandler, Shemilt, Notley and Philip-Smith, who occupied tiny rooms in that strange warren of a building, before the practice was eventually relocated to a state of the art complex in Field Street.

To the left beyond the bollards in the older photograph, stands Cleaver's the builders' merchants, later situated in Eskdaill Street but now extinct. Opposite is the impressive frontage of the Evening Telegraph premises from where the local newspaper was produced for 80 years until the opening of the purpose built site in Northfield Avenue. Also redundant, and awaiting the proposed redevelopment of the area, is the fittingly austere, concrete and glass of the Inland Revenue building.

K

Horsemarket - Bone's and Sloan's

The demolition of the row of shops which faced across the little square now housing the bus shelter and raised flower beds has revealed a changed skyline with the redundant GPO telephone exchange most prominent. The advertising hoardings on Bone's shop on the corner of Bridewell Lane, boldly state the particular virtues of rival detergents, 'Tide, a new weekly wash sensation', and the long forgotten 'Miracle Acdo'.

The less ostentatious premises opposite Sloan's in Dryland Street housed Mildred K Blewitt's Art and Needlework Depository while the tall-chimneyed ediface on the right was formerly the Cross Keys Cafe and Assembly Rooms, originally opened in 1880. It is still possible to make out a faint cross keys motif above the drain pipe on the modern building.

Horsemarket - The Parish Church School

The twin gables of the Parish Church School rise above the high walls surrounding the building known familiarly as 'The School in the Horsemarket'. It closed in 1965 when its respected headteacher, Mr Pat Partridge, staff and pupils moved to the splendid, new Bishop Stopford School in the Headlands. On its eventual demolition in September 1970, Council minutes suggest that 'the site could be used as a temporary car-park'.

The owner of the car parked bottom left may well have been depositing dirty washing at the Kettering Steam Laundry in Church Walk. Bosworth's Motor Cycles occupied the premises behind the No Right Turn sign, while readers may spot the words 'HIPWELL & CO's ALES AND STOUT STORES' still imprinted on the white painted wall of what are now the offices of Richard Norfolk, Solicitors. Beyond Everard and Saltmarsh, Corn Merchants remain two survivors, Dinsdale's Art Shop and The Woolpack pub, (renamed Henry's). Between Bridewell Lane and Dryland Street were the aforesaid Bone's Hardware store and Mildred K Blewitt's needlework shop with Sloan's Drapery, (later Bagshaw's chip shop and currently the 'Tudor Fish Restaurant', no doubt in deference to its black and white facade), occupying the corner opposite.

M

Market Street Corner

Deceptively, very little appears to have changed in the thirty odd years that separate the two photographs. The ultra-modern facade of the Barclays Bank has replaced the attractive Victorian building occupied by William Aber's Walkaround Store, demolished in 1985 and a loss which was much regretted by Kettering people at the time. The building formerly housed Kettering's original Boot's the Chemist shop, before its relocation to the High Street and later to the Newlands Centre. The Royal Hotel is clearly recognisable despite almost continuous remodelling, and the white painted corner shop opposite in West Street, once Poole's tobacconist and confectioners, has had a change of colour but is still operating - unlike several other well known Kettering businesses which occupied the row of shops facing the market place, of which Johnson's Fruiterers, the Parker and Carlton butchery and Silver's the chemist come readily to mind.

N

Hazelwood House

The once handsome, now derelict building in the background is Hazelwood House, situated appropriately in Hazelwood Lane off West Street, until its demolition in 1955. Home to the family of Kettering's famous dissenting Rector, John Maidwell, during the late 17th century, it was the scene of many 'illegal' services held by worshippers determined to be independent of the Church of England and its strictly imposed orthodoxy. Here, on this very spot, we have the meeting place of those splendid fore-runners of the Nonconformist movement which later flourished and gave so much character to the town. The remains of the old structure are sensibly being incorporated into the development currently taking place on the site. The wooden building to the left of the old photograph is the former HQ of the Kettering Sea-Cadets, (HMS Pytchley'), latterly relocated to its present home near the Scouts Woodcroft Centre in London Road.

O

The Lawns

The well appointed development of sheltered accommodation and elderly people's bungalows at the bottom of George Street bears the name of the impressive building which occupied much of the site until its demolition in December 1955. Formerly home to the Loake family, foremost among Kettering's Boot and Shoe manufacturers, it became the Lawn Youth Centre in 1943, when Mr Ernest W Loake presented the premises to the town for the use of the Sea Cadet Corps, the Air Training Corps and the Girls Training Corps. Hundreds attended the handing-over ceremony on July 3rd, when Sir William Dobbie, GCMG, KCB, DSO, the former Governor of Malta, addressed a large gathering on the huge green that gave the building its name. The tennis courts at the back of the house survived long after its demolition, but were eventually built over when the site was tastefully extended in 1991.

The Talbot Inn

Only some 35 years separate these views down Meadow Road, (formerly Gas Street and much earlier the delightfully named Goosepasture Lane), yet were it not for the lone car at the bottom of the hill in the older photograph, they might well be centuries apart. Fred Hefford, the boxing promoter and licensee of the Talbot Inn, and a friend contemplate a pastoral scene in stark contrast to the nineties photograph which shows all too well the complete dominance of the motor car.

Closer examination reveals that the terraced row opposite the pub is in fact derelict and awaiting its demolition in January 1960, to be replaced eventually by the offices of Wilson Browne, solicitors.

Q

Gasholder Meadow Road

This skeletal steel structure was, for many years, a familiar landmark on the site now occupied by the B and Q and Comet superstores on the corner of Meadow Road and Northfield Avenue. In 1834 the Kettering Gas and Coke Company had acquired a quarter of an acre plot on Wyman's meadow and began producing gas in October of that year. Goosepasture Lane forfeited its pastoral identity and was renamed Gas Street, before eventually assuming its present day nomenclature - Meadow Road. A short distance further along Northfield Avenue roughly on the site now occupied by the Lidl supermarket was the Kettering Gas Company employees football ground. Situated as it was alongside the Slade brook, which was prone to flooding, I recall on several occasions seeing just the white tops of the goalposts and crossbar protruding from opposite ends of the lake that was the pitch. The sportsground and its ramshackle grandstand disappeared long before 1966 when operations at the gasworks ceased. Four years later the demolition of the site began, leading to the eventual dismantling of the gasholders.

Wadcroft

Wadcroft was the name given to the area bordered by High Street, Meadow Road, Commercial Road and Trafalgar Road. Its main streets were Walkers Lane, Bellfoundry Lane and Shalom Place and it was one of Kettering's oldest residential and commercial districts. By the fifties many of the properties had become derelict and most were demolished to create the car park at the rear of Woolworths. The large three-storeyed building in the photograph survived as West End Wallpapers before being replaced by the more modern premises now occupied by Tarry's Shoe Store.

Wadcroft Chapel

The chapel of the *Calvinistic (Strict) Baptists,* stood in the part of Wadcroft known as Shalom Place, the most northerly of its three thoroughfares. Originally built in 1868 by a Mr Pain of Great Oakley, the Jehovah Shalom as it was named, eventually became redundant indeed Mr J Fovargue, latterly of the Chrysler Garage in Bayes Street, recalls using his hire car to transport the bride and her father to the last wedding held at the chapel in 1927. Recent research indicates that it ceased to exist as a religious building soon after this date. Nevertheless it continued in serviceable use as indicated by this photograph until it finally disappeared as part of major changes to the area mentioned on the previous page. The white sports car TK 27, pictured alongside the building, and surely a status symbol of its time, belonged to Tony Kay, manager of Alfred Webb's Outfitters, situated opposite Woolworths in Bellfoundry Lane.

Bakehouse Hill

Situated at the junction of High Street, Lower Street and Gold Street, Bakehouse Hill was something of a focal point back in the fifties. Not only shoppers converged on this popular venue, but also traffic using the A6 to Rothwell, Desborough and beyond, and Stamford bound vehicles on the A43. The shop pictured in the older photograph is that of ironmongers, Bell and Billows , whose window displays of air rifles and sheath knives regularly attracted an audience of fascinated schoolboys. Other premises on Bakehouse Hill included Theobald's the bakers, whose halfpenny bread rolls provided essential refreshment on visits to the Saturday morning picture shows, and an office block built in 1897 and incorporating the KICS number 1 store. To the left, in Lower Street, is Boot's the Chemist, relocated from its original position in Market Street, and Civil's grocers who had once occupied premises in Montagu Street, while another interesting frontage belongs to Harry Buttery, one of Kettering's earliest Estate Agents. Bakehouse Hill was demolished to make way for Phase One of the Newborough development, which opened in 1969, and its name was officially abolished by the Council.

THE CENTENARY OF THE EVENING TELEGRAPH

The Kettering Leader and Observer

FRIDAY, OCTOBER 8th, 1897.

LOCAL NOTES.

The principal local event of the week has been the establishment of a daily newspaper for the town and district. The hearty welcome accorded "The Evening Telegraph" affords gratifying evidence that the venture is a timely one, and it has evidently come to stay. The circulation has exceeded the most sanguine expectations, and has embraced nearly all the populous centres of the county. Kettering naturally comes first, but a large sale has also been secured in Northampton, Wellingborough, Rushden, and the numerous villages of the district. "The Evening Telegraph" will be of special value as an advertising medium, seeing that the area in which it circulates is so wide and populous.

The announcement of the birth of the new newspaper, recorded in the *Evening Telegraph's* weekly forerunner, the *Kettering Leader and Observer*.

For almost eighty years, the *Evening Telegraph's* head office and works were in Dryland Street, originally called Workhouse Lane.

> **1897**
> Linotype machines were used for the first time in Kettering to set type for the new evening paper.

> **1899**
> Rotary presses were introduced to print enough papers to cope with demand for news created by the Boer War.

> **1907**
> The first Evening Telegraph was delivered by motor van. Previous distribution had been by train or horse and cart.

Thomas Collings
Baptist minister at Burton Latimer and also managing director of the Northamptonshire Printing and Publishing Company, the first editor of the *Evening Telegraph*.

23

1908
The first photograph appeared, although they did not become a regular feature until the 1920s.

1912
Reporters got their first typewriter. Until then stories had to be written out in longhand before being set in type.

THE GREAT WAR 1914-18

From behind a Co-operative drapery counter at Kettering Mr William Boulter went to World War I, and as Sgt Boulter won the VC.

Evening Telegraph photographer, Spencer Percival, captured raw recruits at Kettering being introduced to the mysteries of puttee drill.

With 73 victims in aerial dogfights Major Edward Mannock VC, a former Wellingborough electrician, was an outstanding air ace.

The celebrated body of local dignitaries and businessmen who ran the *Evening Telegraph* in the twenties.

Delivery vans of the thirties speeded circulation.

The Charter Mayor, Mr JA Gotch, and entourage on ceremonial duty in 1938.

Frank Hutchen
Succeeded Thomas Collings as Managing Editor in 1901 and was, in colleague Tony Ireson's words, '*the on-the-spot presiding genius of the Evening Telegraph until his death in 1942*'.

A scribbled note on the back of this photograph, dated **September 27th 1939,** reads, '*What would Sir Thomas Tresham have said? Rothwell Market House, scheduled as an ancient monument, is now a first aid post protected by sandbags.*'

1940
Evening Telegraph readers donated sufficient money to buy seven Spitfires - a remarkable contribution to the war effort.

Evacuees, bewildered, labelled, gasmasks strung around their necks, pictured arriving at Kettering station in the early days of the war.

The *Pink 'Un*, (1897-1974) RIP, was essential reading for local football fans, particularly in the immediate post-war years when its circulation extended from Luton in the south to Hunstanton in the north-east, and over 50,000 copies were sold every Saturday evening.

Kettering Town Football Club's most famous signing. The great Tommy Lawton joined the Poppies as player-manager on February 2nd 1956, his signature witnessed by club secretary, Frank Summerly, director Reg Tailby, a youthful David Coleman and several million watching the BBC's 'Sportsview' programme.

> **1947**
> East Midland Allied Press - Emap - parent company of the *Evening Telegraph* established under the guidance of managing director R P Winfrey.

R P Winfrey
Son of Sir Richard, the formidable Liberal politician and newspaper tycoon who had successfully transformed the fortunes of the *Evening Telegraph* during his lengthy association with the company as managing director from 1901-1944.

A striking photograph of the Newborough Centre development which began in 1961 with the demolition of these characteristic buildings of old Kettering, notably Billson's corner at the back of Bakehouse Hill.

Ron Howe

Ron came to Kettering as editor of the Evening Telegraph and its sister title the Northamptonshire Advertsier in 1960. During his 13 years in Kettering he became Editor in Chief of Northamptonshire Newspapers.

1976

The Evening Telegraph moved its headquarters from Dryland Street to Northfield Avenue where a new offset press enabled experiments with colour to begin.

The new premises in Northfield Avenue

News of the proposed closure of the Corby steelworks, revealed in the *Evening Telegraph* early in 1979, began a year of industrial protest including a mass march through the town by steelmen and their supporters on September 20th. Economic recovery after the shock of losing its biggest employer was recognised eleven years later in a special E T supplement, '*Corby: Too Proud to Die*'.

Ron Hunt

Led the *Evening Telegraph* into the nineteen eighties, successfully combining popularity with the community and considerable journalistic expertise.

The Two Tonys
Kettering born and raised, two Evening Telegraph journalists who are justly credited with promoting and stimulating widespread interest in the town's colourful past through their publications.

Tony Ireson
'Old Kettering and its Defenders'
'Old Kettering - A View from the Thirties'
Books 1 - 4

Tony Smith
'Kettering Revisited'
'The Kettering Album - More pictures from the Past'

The Team of '87
Editor Paul Deal, general manager Martin Price and staff, pictured on the Northfield Avenue site in September 1987.

Looking to the Future

The Evening Telegraph is proud of its past and the service it has given to the communities it covers. But as we enter the next era in the newspapers history we look forward to the many challenges ahead - including publishing next year from brand new headquarters on Rothwell Road, a gateway site into Kettering near the A14.

Some features are already planned. The Millenium celebrations will probably prove to be the next major landmark event covered in our pages. We also await the opening of the Centenary Wing, housing a new cancer care unit at Kettering General Hospital, paid for through the proceeds of our 100th birthday fund-raising appeal.

Whatever the future holds, one thing is certain. The Evening Telegraph will continue to maintain its proud tradition in being the first to bring its readers the news.

David Rowell

David Rowell - August 1997
Editor-in-Chief

Kettering General Hospital
1897   Centenary   1997

The stone facade of Kettering General Hospital in Rothwell Road, illustrated by local artist, poet and hairdresser, George Harrison, to celebrate the opening of the building in the autumn of 1897.

An early photograph of members of the staff. Central figures, seated, Dr J Allison and the first Matron, Miss G Hick.

The first Evening Telegraph report to extend to more than a few paragraphs, and the first to be illustrated with a large picture, was the opening of the Kettering General Hospital.

Kettering was growing so rapidly in the latter part of the century that, with the nearest hospital situated at Northampton, it was apparent that the town required its own medical facility. In 1891 a local Nursing Association revived plans for a cottage hospital, originally planned four years earlier to mark Queen Victoria's Golden Jubilee. The scheme received influential backing, notably from Mr J T Stockburn, who offered £500 towards the project and the Duke of Buccleuch, who donated a three acre site.

Architect J A Gotch drew up plans and in 1895 the newly formed hospital committee, with Stockburn as chairman, put these out to tender. Seven quotations were received and the lowest, £5,575 submitted by Alfred Barlow, was accepted. The foundation stone was laid by the Duchess of Buccleuch the following year, and in 1897 the building was officially opened.

HOSPITAL BUILT FOR £5,575

Dr Leslie Winter Dryland
1834-1906
Honorary surgeon to the
Kettering General Hospital

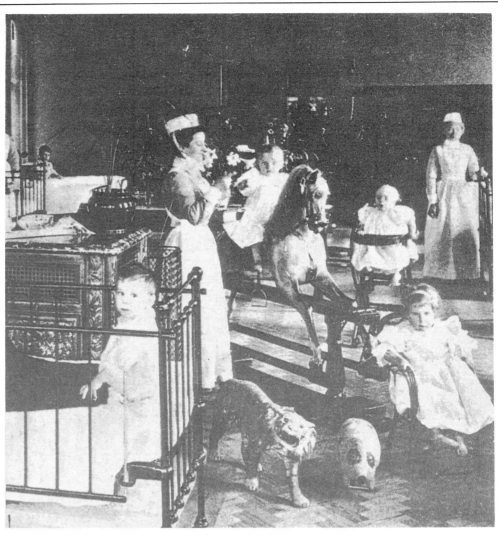

Dr Harold Cooper Pretty
1876-1952
Honorary Medical Officer to
Kettering General Hospital

This photograph of the children's ward, dating from before the
outbreak of the First World War, beautifully captures the
atmosphere of the period.

Dr Frank Radcliffe
1907-1977
Architect and Surgeon in
charge of the casualty unit,
the first of its type in the
country

A patient receives treatment under the recently installed heat lamps
in the Physiotherapy Department, 1924.

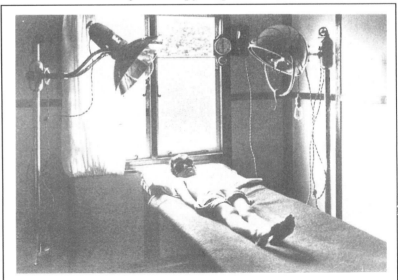

From a Distance

An aerial view of the hospital showing the Spencer and Buccleuch wards, which were added to the original building in 1902 increasing the number of beds available to fifty eight.

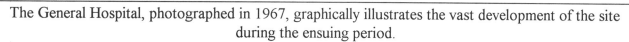

The General Hospital, photographed in 1967, graphically illustrates the vast development of the site during the ensuing period.

Innovation and Expansion

The Post Graduate Medical Centre, opened in 1976 by H R H the Duchess of Gloucester who is pictured alongside Mr Hutchinson, Chairman of the Hospital trustees.

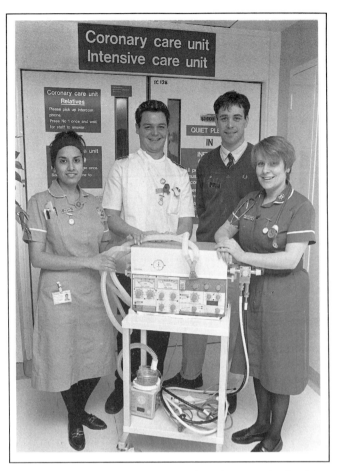

Staff from the Coronary care unit, photographed with a new ventilating machine, in November 1993.

A multi-storeyed concrete and glass, ward complex dating from the nineteen eighties.

Today, Kettering General Hospital employs 2,380 members of staff including 200 doctors. It cares for approximately 50,000 patients per annum through its Accident and Emergency Department, treats 55,000 patients on an in-patient or day case basis and cares for in excess of 180,000 patients each year through its Outpatient Department.

Old Grammar School

This building, with its fine sandstone Victorian Gothic ediface, was completed in 1856 to replace the former and totally inadequate, thatched school premises. It was demolished on the morning of Sunday, November 29th, 1964. Conservationists among newcomers to the town may well wonder how so grand a building could be sacrificed so easily to the developers' plans. But even such doughty campaigners as Tony Ireson were stunned by the swift, almost clandestine, action of the authorities in carrying out the demolition, which left no opportunity for protest. The action led directly to the formation of the Kettering Civic Society, which has continued to fight valiantly against similar acts of vandalism to this day. The school had ceased to house pupils in 1913 with the opening of the new building in Bowling Green Road. For over twenty years it was home and surgery to Dr Daniel Drake-Lee, father of William, before becoming local council offices. Indeed in 1961 I remember being interviewed there for a summer holiday job in the Parks Department, while a student at Teacher Training College in London. History was repeated shortly after this when the Grammar and High schools vacated the Bowling Green Road premises for new accommodation in Windmill Avenue and Lewis Road, enabling the entire Borough Council staff to occupy the building. The gateway on the right was the entrance to the Crown Brewery, once owned by the Elworthy family, who conducted their business on the site from the late nineteenth century until Marston, Thompson and Evershed acquired the premises in 1931. The words Marston's Burton Ales can be read on the open wooden gate leading to the brewery yard.

Savoy/Ohio

Situated in Russell Street, Kettering's only surviving cinema, now known as the Ohio, was looking rather run down when this photograph was taken in the late fifties. A poster over the entrance advertises Ted Heath and his Music, recalling the glory days

when, as the Avenue Theatre and later the Coliseum, it had attracted top acts from the world of Music Hall. The Savoy rose from the ashes after fire destroyed the original building back in 1938, and continued to present both films and concerts for many years after the war. One local celebrity has good reason to thank the Savoy's 'Carrol Levis Discovery Show' for setting him on his way to stardom - Rothwell born Jim Smith, or Jim Dale as he is now more familiarly known. Just 44 years ago Kettering film goers were spoilt for choice as the ET *Lets Go To The Pictures* advertisement from February 1953 indicates.

The Kettering Ohio closed on Wednesday 30th July 1997 during the final drafting of this text, ending over 70 years of cinema in the town.

Empire Cinema

By the early fifties the *Empire* in Eskdaill Street was a sad relic of the splendidly intimate little cinema built and opened in 1920 by a company headed by Harry Bamford, whose photographer's shop stood on the site now occupied by Glover's cycles. With antique lamps for house lighting, and plush red seats, including the notoriously daring double-seats for 'courting' couples, in its heyday it must have provided a luxurious venue for film-goers. I can only recall one visit to the 'flea-pit', as it had become widely known in my youth, for a programme which included an *'Old Mother Riley'* film and newsreel coverage of *Royal Tan* winning the 1954 *'Grand National'*. It must have been one of the last shows staged at the cinema as it closed later that year.

Now a motor Exhaust and Silencer Centre, the *Empire's* frontage remains virtually unchanged, although it now has a pitched roof, the impressive arched entrance has been blocked off and its sign painted over.

Odeon

The Odeon was the final incarnation of the Victoria Hall, originally opened in 1888 in Gold Street as a multi-purpose entertainment centre for the people of the town. From 1907-1920 it was a full-time professional theatre before responding to the popular trend and becoming a cinema. Acquired by the Odeon chain in the early thirties, the Victorian interior was remodelled by local builders, OP Drever, and the stone frontage replaced by the ubiquitous 'picturehouse' style shown in the photograph. As a child I joined the hundreds of Odeon Club members who *'went along on Saturday morning, greeting everybody with a smile'*, to cheer eponymous heroes, Hopalong Cassidy and Flash Gordon. The film 'Sapphire', advertised in the photograph starring Nigel Patrick and Michael Craig, was among the last to be shown at the cinema which closed in 1960. It was used, briefly, for bingo sessions, and my solitary act of civil disobedience was to join friends in the early hours of a summer Sunday in 1961 to mount 'Ban the Bingo - Give us back our cinema', posters all over the entrance. It was a somewhat feeble gesture, dismissed in the press as 'mindless vandalism'. Those words, however, would be better attributed to the wholesale destruction of the Old Post Office buildings and the adjoining Odeon and Crown Inn Brewery premises in the mid-seventies. Like many others who now bemoan the loss of so many of Kettering's old buildings I can only admire the largely frustrated efforts of their 'Defenders', so vividly described in Tony Ireson's fine book, and wish I had done more to support their campaign. As the older photograph reveals, the shops to the immediate right of the cinema, now part of the row leading to the entrance to the Newlands centre, were formerly occupied by Millers, gown specialists, and George Mason, the grocers.

Granada

Originally the Regal, this splendid example of Art Deco style architecture was opened on Boxing Day, 1938. By the early fifties it had become the Granada, and was probably the most popular cinema in the town, (except among we Saturday morning Odeonites who regarded the rival 'Kettering Grenadiers' as an alien breed). I can clearly remember queues for the Saturday evening programme stretching along the High Street and down Meadow Road almost as far as Frederick Charter's furniture store. Most cinemas in those days offered a frequent change of programme - there was the Monday, Tuesday, Wednesday bill, a different Thursday, Friday, Saturday show, and yet another on Sundays. With its 'Miss Candy' sweet shop, snack bar, foyer coke machine, plush carpets and smart first floor restaurant it was much more than just a picture-house. The regular Bandshows of the early sixties brought many leading pop stars to the town, and featured on the advertising display above the entrance are 'The Senators', a top local group of the day. To the left of the cinema we can see part of the frontage of Timpson's shoe shop, and above that, the office windows of Cattell and Chater, Chartered Accountants.

Today Granada has become Gala - a popular venue for bingo devotees.

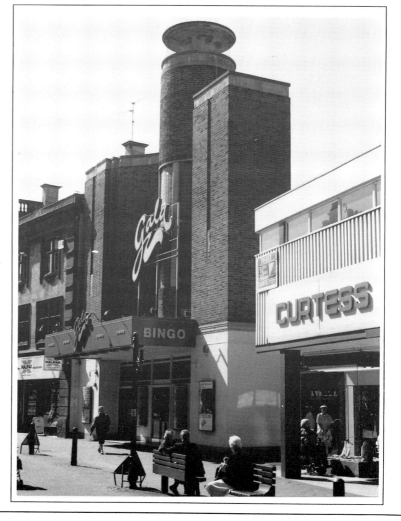

Gaumont

Photographed in 1959, the year of its closure, when showing a double bill of 'Al Capone', starring Rod Steiger, and 'Wolf Larsen' with Peter Graves. Built in 1913 as the Pavilion, it was referred to affectionately as the 'Pav' by many Kettering folk long after its name changed to the rather less than splendid Gaumont. The space to the left of the cinema was originally the site of the New White Horse Inn, (not to be confused with the Old White Horse Inn which stood farther along the High Street and is now occupied by Burton's the Tailor). In 1953, an aspiring young actress called Joan Collins re-opened the cinema after redecoration, but just seven years later it was demolished to make way for the row of shops that now occupy the site in the High Street.

The Palace Cinema, Burton Latimer

The earlier photograph of the entrance to the Palace cinema recalls the days when even the smaller towns in the area had their own picture-houses. Desborough had the Ritz, Finedon the Star and Raunds the Carlton. The film advertised, 'Serious Charge', starring Anthony Quayle and Andrew Ray, dates the photograph from 1959, for as pop music fans will readily remember, it also featured the young Cliff Richard, and his hit song of that year, 'Living Doll'.

The Palace has had a chequered history since those days of long queues and crowded auditoriums. With the increasing popularity of television, it closed and remained so for several years before a gallant attempt at re-opening in the eighties re-christened 'Bentley's'. Despite showing such excellent films as 'The Mission', 'Mona Lisa' and 'Crocodile Dundee' - which represented the rather minimal extent of Robert Mercer's and my support for the venture - the rising expectations and growing sophistication of cinema audiences, coupled with a disastrous fire, eventually led to its inevitable demise. I recall being more than a little exasperated during the showing of 'Mona Lisa, by the poor synchronisation which caused most of Cathy Tyson's words to be spoken by Bob Hoskins. But perhaps that was just a bad night. Today's audiences expect the comparative luxury, wide choice and state of the art facilities of the multi-screen complexes often built, like the one currently under construction near the A14, in an out of town Venture Park.

Kettering Cooperative Boot and Shoe Manufacturing Society, Havelock Street and Nelson Street corner.

Inhabitants of the block of smart flats now occupying the site of the old 'Holyoake' factory in Havelock Street may be unaware of its unique place in Kettering's history. It is hardly surprising that the Cooperative movement, whose many enterprises flourished so vigorously in the town for over a hundred years, should extend its activities to the boot and shoe trade. In 1896 the imposing building was acquired to cope with burgeoning demand, workers manufacturing quality footwear under the Holyoake brand name, marked with the oak leaf motif and slogan 'Justice for all'.

The blind protruding on the bottom left of the older photograph was from Jack Pettit's butcher's shop and the little boys hurrying home from Park Road school in neighbouring Wood Street are passing Joan Spurr's ladies hairdresser's.

Timpson's Factory, Bath Road

William Timpson Limited's splendid factory was built in 1922 to replace the original premises in Market Street, now occupied by the Yorkshire Bank. By 1956, when this photograph was taken, it employed hundreds of boot and shoe workers who produced some 20,000 pairs a week, supplying the great chain of family owned shops throughout the country and abroad. The building was a well known landmark throughout my childhood, especially on winter evenings when, with lights blazing through its rows of huge windows, it resembled nothing less than a mighty ocean liner moored beyond the North Park cricket field. It closed in 1972 but was then acquired, first by the British Shoe Corporation and subsequently the Burlington International Group, which collapsed into receivership in 1992. After standing derelict for several years the model factory, a symbol of the town's great shoemaking heritage, was finally demolished in the summer of 1996. I suspect that many Kettering people, for whom the great building was so familiar a feature will, like me, continue to be totally disorientated when passing the Burghley Gardens site for many years to come.

London Road Terrace

This long terraced row, which extended down from Wallis's garage, (originally the Pytchley Auto Car Company and now Cooper Armstrong), on the corner of London Road and the Grove, to the large house opposite St Mary's hospital, was demolished in 1965. The signs hanging to the left of the garage display allegiance to both the RAC and AA, while the showroom advertises the latest Wolesley and Morris motor cars. At the centre of the row of ironstone houses with identical white painted lintels, the Walls ice cream sign denotes the frontage of Sumpter's shop. (Older readers may recall the days when the ice cream was actually made in a barn at the back of the building). Much of the site is now occupied by Harry Potter House, sheltered accommodation for the elderly, named after the influential local councillor, former mayor, and manager during the thirties of the Union Co-operative Boot and Shoe factory in Regent Street.

Deeble Road

The map of Kettering in the mid fifties shows a vast swathe of virgin territory extending between the Ise brook and Warkton Lane. Building ends with the houses in Cheyne Walk, Valley Walk and Margaret Road. East Avenue peters out into a track that leads down to the bridge across the brook and Deeble Road ends abruptly just beyond the playing field behind Southgate Drive. The older photograph, looking back towards the town, was taken in the late sixties when development began to the east of the Ise, culminating in one of Britain's largest private housing estates.

Kettering Mill

Standing in splendid isolation in the Ise valley, Kettering Mill, although still occupied, had already been redundant for many years when this photograph was taken in the late fifties. The building was a familiar landmark for generations of schoolboys undergoing the painful winter ritual of cross-country running. For years as an uncnlightened youngster I thought this route from the old Grammar School playing field in London Road, along Windmill Avenue, down the track past the mill, across the valley and back via the lane through Barton Hall, was actually called the 'milk-horse'!

It is very difficult today to visualise the actual location that these buildings occupied in the valley. Taking the photograph one morning in early spring we had a natural inclination to place the site of the mill much closer to the river than it actually was, but as this was re-routed some distance to the east during the thirties, *(see map page iv)*, the position of the building was in fact closer to the new houses off East Avenue. Kettering born and raised Norman Neal, pictured with truck in the later photo, tended one of the many garden-fields that, together with several rubbish dumps, originally occupied much of the west bank of the Ise between Deeble Road, Valley Walk and Margaret Road. He recalls the Amos family living at Mill House during the forties, and the outbuildings being used as a training gym for young boxers.

Prefabs Highfield Road

Looking up Highfield Road towards the Oval, modern three-storeyed flats have now replaced that remarkable housing innovation, the prefab. Originally erected in 1946 to cope with an increased demand after the second world war, these 'temporary' buildings had an estimated lifespan of ten years. In the event they far exceeded their sell-by date and it was 1971 before occupants were finally rehoused. Long time residents expressed mixed feelings about leaving. Some felt a sentimental attachment to the properties praising their well constructed if basic design and generous gardens, but most referred to a susceptibility to damp, difficulties in keeping warm in winter and unbearable heat in summer. Behind the prefabs on the left of the older photograph lies Highfields Primary school, opened in 1951 under the idiosyncratic headship of J L Carr, artist, cartographer and author, twice short-listed for the Booker Prize. The buildings to the right front the network of garden-fields that once stretched down to the brook at the back of Springfield Road. The present road is strewn with calming humps - a deterrent to traffic using the road as a short cut to the A509.

Cranford Station

Before the Beeching Act of 1963 brought draconian changes to the national network, distinctive station buildings like the one pictured at Cranford could be found at regular intervals along the county's railway lines. Beautifully maintained, their platforms hosed and swept, waiting-room fires glowing, embankments lovingly tended like garden plots, '*grateful and comforting*' like the Epps's cocoa advertised on the station wall, they were a picturesque feature of post-war Britain.

Pre-dating Beeching by some years, the last passenger train stopped at Cranford station *en-route* to Cambridge on June 13th 1959. Today, like the beverage itself, many have passed into oblivion or lie abandoned and derelict. Some however have escaped that fate, as here the building has been successfully converted into a highly desirable home. The old platform wall provides an ideal raised bed and a lawn fills the space originally occupied by the railway track.

Storefield Cottages

These photographs of Storefield Cottages, on the A 6003 between Kettering and Corby, provide graphic evidence of the impact of motor transport on the local landscape over the past forty years. In the earlier scene workmen are using primitive machinery to construct the first 'relief' road, originally built to carry a rapidly increasing traffic flow northbound from Kettering. Much to the delight of the residents of the cottages, another carriageway was added later some distance to the west, providing welcome respite from the rush of vehicles past their front doors. The original road can be seen winding its way up the hill through the trees on the right of the current photograph. The imposing bridge which spans the road at this point once carried a busy railway line from Kettering to Corby. Further proof, if it was needed, of changed priorities.

In stark contrast to the proliferation of signs that dominate the present view, the old photograph shows a single modest finger-post marking the way to Rushton. A rural invitation echoing a time when more sedate perambulations actually gave travellers an opportunity to respond and decide where they were going. Are we perhaps losing *our* sense of direction?

The Spread Eagle, Oakley Hay

This view of the Spread Eagle pub at Oakley Hay, dating from the late fifties, had probably remained unchanged for generations. The tree framed cluster of buildings nestling at the bottom of the lane, the solitary overalled workman, kneeling amongst the cow parsley, or 'kek' as we always called it, lend a distinctly timeless quality.

But how things change. A plastic bollard indicates the short route to the hostelry from the busy road carrying speeding traffic towards the centre of Corby. Directly behind the pub on the sprawling Oakley Hay industrial estate stands a massive white painted, flat roofed factory, home to Quebecor Printing (UK) Plc. Corby continues to sprawl south towards Kettering, determined it seems to fulfil my mother's unlikely prophecy made over thirty years ago that the two towns would eventually join.

Stephenson Way, Corby

Few pictures tell the story of Corby's recent past more dramatically than these photographs. Stephenson Way, formerly overshadowed by the giant superstructure of the blast furnaces, has been transformed into a typical suburban street, all signs of the town's industrial past extinguished. From the arrival of Scottish firm, Stewart and Lloyds, in the thirties until its partial closure almost fifty years later, the steelworks had been the main employer for thousands of workers in the locality. In the short period of expansion before the second world war Corby grew from a village of around 1,500 people into a town of 10,000. This expansion was accelerated from 1950 following its designated status as one of the first post-war New Towns and a population target of 55,000 was reached by 1977. The vulnerability of a one industry town was graphically demonstrated by a decline in the demand for steel and recovery has been an expensive process both in economic and human terms.

The large building just visible on the immediate left is the old Odeon cinema, now relegated to the role of furniture warehouse, while its adjacent parade of shops houses only Murdoch's general store.

Shops, Occupation Road, Corby.

The rather unusual row of shops in Occupation Road Corby provided essential services for local residents of the new town during the fifties. The premises pictured, The Glebe fruit and confectionery stores, Allan's bakery, Murdoch the newsagent, Martin's bookmakers and Cabe's fish shop, occupied Nissen type buildings separated by huge wooden gates allowing access for deliveries.

At first glance there is little to link the present parade, fronted by a well used service road, with the earlier view. Imaginative reconstruction has successfully utilised the space between the buildings to provide double-fronted premises now offering a wide variety of products ranging from security systems to video cassettes. Perhaps significantly, of the five original businesses in the row, only Martin's the bookmakers continues to operate from the site. On the extreme left, the tower of Our Lady of Walsingham RC Church rises behind a more conventional shop building, currently The Victoria Wine Stores and formerly Charles off-licence.

Harringworth School

This evocative view from the fifties shows children dancing, hand-in-hand in a ring, on the school playground before the splendid backdrop of the Harringworth viaduct.

In common with many similar small schools, Harringworth gradually became unviable as the number of pupils fell, costs escalated and educational priorities changed, leading to closure on July 22nd 1965.

In more recent years many local villages have campaigned successfully to keep their schools open, recognising that closure often heralds the disintegration of community life. However, the counter argument, citing cold economic facts and the real need to provide today's children with the appropriate facilities to meet current curricular expectations, is a powerful one and it remains to be seen if the smaller schools are able to continue into the next century.

As you see, Harringworth school, largely unchanged in forty years, has been converted into the village hall, while the distant railway viaduct - its 82 arches built with over 20 million bricks and opened in 1879 to carry the Kettering to Melton Mowbray line threequarters of a mile across the Welland valley - is now restricted to freight traffic, although enthusiasts can take advantage of an occasional Sunday passenger service when track repairs necessitate the re-routing of the Kettering to Leicester line.

Blatherwycke Hall

This pleasant glade below, bathed in spring sunshine, betrays no sign of the great Georgian mansion that occupied the site at Blatherwycke for over two hundred years. The once grand house, pictured above shortly before it was demolished in 1948, was home to the Stafford O'Brien family, and had itself replaced a Tudor manor house pulled down in the middle of the eighteenth century. A celebrated occupant of that original house was Sir Humphrey Stafford, who in 1570 began the construction of nearby Kirby Hall. The Staffords were later united in marriage with the Irish O'Briens, and a love-knot linking the initials of the two families can be seen inscribed on the walls of several properties in the village.

While the redundant church of the Holy Trinity contains many splendid memorials to their forebears, the last surviving members of the family, spinster sisters Matilda Finola and Lucy Mary, lie buried side by side in the overgrown graveyard. They died well into their eighties, within months of each other, ending a long and eventful companionship that had seen the world profoundly altered since the 'heady days' of their youth before the First World War.

The Old Friar, Twywell

That unlikely status symbol of the nineteen nineties, the four wheel drive vehicle, occupies a prime position amid the picnic tables on the forecourt of the Old Friar pub at Twywell. Almost every added feature of the modern building, from the large lettered name board blazoned across the front, to the satellite dish providing endless helpings of Sky Sport, reflects the changes that have enabled the more enterprising village pubs to survive. What would the flat capped villager, pint and pipe in hand, and his demure wife have made of it all?

Gone are the star shaped signs advertising the Northampton Brewery Company, *'There's none so fair as can compare with a bottle of NBC'.*

Tetley's bitter now courses through the pipes, and a hot and cold carvery, a la carte bar snacks and vegetarian meals have replaced the authentic ploughman's lunch.

However, the large front entrance appears welcoming and the modern toilet facilities are doubtless considerably more comfortable than the horrors that might be concealed behind the door marked 'Gentlemen' on the extreme right of the older photograph.

Where are they?

Like many other clues to Kettering's past, the views depicted in these two photographs are either tucked away in a side street or appear high above the eye line and can easily be missed by the casual passer-by.

In his informative pamphlet, *'An Off-beat look at Kettering'*, local historian, Allah Buksh lists a number of such significant historical 'curiosities' to be unearthed on a leisurely walk around the town's back streets.

Answers on page 56.

INDEX

Bakehouse Hill 22
Blatherwycke Hall 52

Cinemas, Empire 35
    Gaumont 38
    Granada 37
    Odeon 36
Burton Latimer, Palace 39
    Savoy/Ohio 34

Corby 49, 50
Cranford Station 46

Deeble Road 43
Dryland Street 12, 23

Ebenezer Place 11
Eskdaill Street 9
Evening Telegraph 23-28

Field Street Avenue 5

Gasholder, Meadow Road 19

Harringworth School 51
Havelock Street 40
Hazelwood House 16
Highfield Road, prefabs 45
Horsemarket 13, 14

Jasmine House 1

Kettering Co-op Boot & Shoe 40
Kettering General Hospital 29-32
Kettering Mill 44
Kettering Textiles 4

London Road Terrace 42
Lower Street Triangle 2, 3
Lawns, The 17

Montagu Corner 10
Market Street Corner 15
Meadow Road 19

Nelson Street 40
Newborough Centre 26
Newland Street 7
Northfield Avenue 27
Northall Street 6

Oakley Hay, *Spread Eagle* 48
Occupation Road Shops 50
Old Grammar School 33

Rothwell, Market House 25

St Andrew's Street 8, 9
Stephenson Way, Corby 49
Storefield Cottages 47

Talbot Inn 18
Timpson's Shoe Factory 41
Twywell, *Old Friar* 53

Wadcroft 20
Wadcroft Chapel 21

BIBLIOGRAPHY

Old Kettering and its Defenders   Tony Ireson
Kettering - A View From the Thirties Books 1-4   Tony Ireson
Kettering Revisited   Tony Smith
The Kettering Album - More Pictures From the Past   Tony Smith
Pictorial History of Kettering   Rotary Club of Kettering Huxloe
Northamptonshire Life 1914-39   R L Greenall
Kettering Revisited - Compilation Edition 1984   Kettering Civic Society
A Portrait of Kettering in the Age of Reform   L Partridge
Kelly's Directory 1914 and 1940 Editions
Northamptonshire Past and Present   Northamptonshire Record Society

Where Are They Now?

A.   The clasped hands, and the motto 'Justice to all', can be seen above the entrance to the Classic Homes warehouse in Havelock Street. Dated 1890, the building was originally erected to house the Kettering Cooperative Boot and Shoe Manufacturing Society factory before its move just four years later to a larger premises further down the same street.

B.   This advertisement for Kettering's last public blacksmith and farrier can be found in the lane leading off Dalkeith Place by the Central Motors garage.